DATE DUE		
JY 30 '99		
NO 03 '99		
JA 04 '00		

21750
6.95

J
796.4
Per

Percefull, Aaron W.
      Gymnastics

GYM NASTICS

Aaron W.
Percefull

AN EASY-READ
SPORTS BOOK

FRANKLIN WATTS

NEW YORK/LONDON

TORONTO/SYDNEY

1982

TO JANE, WITH THANKS

Reading Level 2.6 Spache Revised Formula

Photographs courtesy of:
U.S. Gymnastics Federation: pp. 1, 4, 7, 9, 16, 17,
18, 22, 25, 26, 30, 33, 34, 38, 41, 45; Monkmeyer
Press Photo: p. 10; United Press International:
pp. 13, 42; Sports Photo File: p. 14; Kathryn
Dudek/Photo News: pp. 21, 29, 37.

Library of Congress Cataloging in Publication Data

Percefull, Aaron W.
   Gymnastics.

   (An Easy-to-read sports book)
   Includes index.

   Summary: An introduction to gymnastics, with
advice on safety and training, descriptions
of the competitive events, and a glossary.

   1. Gymnastics—Juvenile literature.
[1. Gymnastics] I. Title. II. Series.
GV461.P45   796.4'1   81-22021
ISBN 0-531-04377-0   AACR2

CONTENTS

WHAT IS GYMNASTICS?

Can you stand on your head? It's hard to balance upside down. Did you ever swing from a tree? It's hard to hold on when you go fast. Gymnasts learn balance and swing.

Did you ever do a somersault just for fun? Gymnastics is fun. It makes you feel good. It makes you feel almost like you are flying.

People have been flip-flopping around for thousands of years. The Chinese did it first. They are still great acrobats. Their tumbling tricks are daring and thrilling.

The Greeks had tumbling at the first Olympics. That was in 776 B.C. Men came from all over to compete in those games. They ran and jumped, wrestled and tumbled.

But the Romans did away with the Olympics. Gymnastics barely survived after that. Traveling actors performed acrobatics to make money. Court jesters were expected to be good tumblers.

Gymnastics did not return as a sport until 1811. Then a German man opened a gymnastics school. His name was Friedrich Jahn. He wanted to make young Germans strong.

Mr. Jahn made up new equipment to help train his students. The parallel bars were his idea. So were the high bar and the rings. He improved the pommel horse. He encouraged his pupils to invent new tricks on the apparatus. Mr. Jahn is the father of modern gymnastics.

Modern gymnastics is six events for boys. They include floor exercises and work on the pommel horse, the rings, the vault, the parallel bars, and the high bar.

Girls have four events. They do floor exercises as well as routines on the balance beam, vault, and uneven parallel bars.

Boys and girls have only two events in common. They are the floor exercises and the vault.

Peter Vidmar performs an L-seat on the parallel bars.

WHAT TO WEAR

Gymnasts are always on the move. So they must wear clothes that let them move. For practice, boys usually wear gym shorts and a T-shirt. Sweat pants are good, too. They protect the legs during high bar work.

Girls can wear gym shorts and a T-shirt. But most girls like leotards and tights.

Gymnasts wear many different things on their feet. Some prefer to go barefoot. Some wear socks. Many like gymnastics slippers. They are leather and don't weigh much. The soles won't slip. Sneakers are not good because they are too heavy.

You will see gymnasts wearing hand grips. Grips protect the hands. They cut down on blisters. But grips are not for beginners. Beginners have soft hands. Their hands must become hardened. They have to get calluses. Then they can wear grips.

SAFETY

Never wear jewelry when working out. That includes watches and rings. Long hair should be pulled back. You don't want it flying in your face. And don't chew gum! You could bite your tongue.

Don't train alone. Make sure your coach is watching you. Do exactly what your coach says. Don't be a show-off. Accidents can happen. Play it safe. You will have more fun.

A gymnast checks her hand grips before mounting the uneven bars.

THE WARM-UP

Always warm up before practice. Cold muscles and joints do not work well. It is easy to pull a cold muscle.

Gymnasts must be strong and limber. The warm-up helps you be both. Are your muscles weak? Your coach may want to strengthen them. You can do sit-ups for your stomach muscles. (Always do sit-ups with knees bent. It is easier on the back.) A strong stomach is important. You can't do an L-seat without it.

Chins help strengthen your back. Push-ups are good for the chest and shoulders. So are dips on the parallel bars. Again, do what you can. You will get stronger.

**Stretching exercises
help to limber up the body.**

Stretching is *very* important. Some people are naturally limber. Most people are not. Daily stretching will make you limber.

Follow your coach's instructions. The coach will teach you ways to stretch every muscle. Remember, never force a stretch. If it hurts, stop! Don't pull hard or bounce up and down. You may over-stretch. Let your own weight pull you.

Your coach will help with the backbend. Arch your back. Keep your hands *and* feet flat on the mat. Do not go up on your toes. Try to place your shoulders over your hands. Your coach will lift the middle of your back from above. Soon your shoulders will loosen up.

Never skip your warm-up. If you come late to practice, do your whole warm-up. That way you won't pull a muscle.

**Tracee Talavera's coach
checks Tracee's feet
for proper positioning.**

Tumbling is good practice for gymnasts.

TUMBLING AND FLOOR EXERCISES

Good tumblers make good gymnasts. That is why coaches stress tumbling. It keeps you limber and makes you strong.

Tumbling is done on long mats. Each person takes a turn on the mat. The coach will tell you what to do. The coach may say: "Front rolls. Go!" The first person does rolls down the mat. Then the second person is up. Soon the last person finishes. Then the coach may say: "Back rolls. Go!" Everyone does back rolls in turn.

Cartwheels look easy. They are not. You will need to practice. One day you will do a cartwheel.

Before long you will know many tricks. You can put the tricks together. They will make a routine. That is what floor exercises are. They are tumbling routines put together.

In competition, both boys and girls do floor exercises. Girls do them to music. They combine dance with tumbling. They move to the music. They try to show what the music is saying and what they feel.

Kris Montera (right) shows a dance movement, and Scott Johnson (facing page) pauses.

Boys do not use music. Their routines stress strength and speed.

In competition, floor exercises tell a lot. They tell how a gymnast will do in the other events. Why? The floor exercises are used in other events. Handstands are done on the floor. They are done on the rings. They are done on the parallel bars. Cartwheels are done on the floor. They are also done on the balance beam. Floor exercises get used everywhere.

17

THE BALANCE BEAM

The crowd becomes silent. A young girl steps forward. She composes herself. Suddenly she mounts the apparatus. It's a mere sliver of wood called the balance beam. It is only 4 inches (10 cm) wide. The gymnast does leaps and rolls. She does cartwheels and walkovers. The crowd is hushed. One false move and it is 4 feet (1.2 m) to the floor.

Beam work is very demanding. It takes concentration. It takes patience. It takes courage. Most of the moves are familiar. The same moves are done on the floor. Leaps, turns, rolls, cartwheels, and walkovers can all be done on the beam. They may seem simple on the floor. On the beam they aren't.

Tina Herman does a back flip on the balance beam.

Even walking is difficult on the beam. Your coach will spot you by holding your hand as you walk. You use a low beam with lots of mats around. Your coach might say: "Point your toes. Step on the ball of your foot. Look up."

Your body will be stiff at first. Once you learn to balance, you will loosen up. Remember, the beam is not going anywhere. *You* are! Before long, you will walk with confidence. The beam will seem a mile wide.

Some girls practice at home. They use a two-by-four on the floor. The 4-inch (10-cm) side is about as wide as a beam.

Beam routines are delicate and graceful. The tricks must flow smoothly, one after another. Judges give high points for smooth routines.

A young gymnast poses gracefully on the beam.

THE VAULT

Vaults are quick. They are over before you know it. The gymnast comes up to the line. Zoom! He runs toward the vaulting horse. He hits the springboard with his feet. Up he goes, touching the horse for a split second. Then he is high in the air. In a flash he has done a Tsukahara. (That is a very hard vault.) He lands. It's a firm landing. He doesn't lurch forward. His arms are outstretched above him. His arms form a *V*. He hopes the *V* is for *victory*. He smiles. The whole vault took him two seconds.

Peter Korman prepares to land after a thrilling vault.

Both boys and girls vault. The events are very similar. The horse is a little lower for the girls. Also, girls vault across the width of the horse. Boys vault across the length.

But boys and girls must learn the same techniques. Everyone starts by learning to run. The run before a vault is very controlled. The vaulter knows every step and builds up great speed. You will learn to measure your run and make it exact.

The springboard is not very springy. It is not like a diving board. You don't jump right on it. You almost skim over it. It gives you a small lift up. Practice using the springboard. Learn to jump over rolled-up mats.

**Ron Galimore
has just left
the springboard.**

24

Soon you will learn to jump onto the horse. Your hands make contact first. Then your feet touch. You are in a squat position. You jump off the horse. There is a crash mat on the other side. With practice, your Squat Vault will improve. Your hands will touch the horse briefly. Your feet won't touch at all.

In contests, vaulting isn't scored like other events. The other events are made up of lots of tricks put together. Vaulting is just one, quick trick. Each vault has its own value. The easiest vault is worth 7.0 points. The hardest vault is worth 10.0. The run is not judged. But the run creates the height of the vault. The height *is* judged. So is the landing. But the trick is most important of all.

Marcia Frederick does a back flip off the vaulting horse.

THE UNEVEN PARALLEL BARS

The young gymnast does a vaulting mount to the bars. She glides to the upper bar and casts off. She swings down fast. Thwack! She hits the lower bar with her thighs. It sounds like it hurts, but it doesn't. She swings and circles without a break. She changes directions. Now she flies off the top bar. After two twists she lands. It's a wonderful dismount!

Routines on the uneven parallel bars are exciting to watch. They are fast-moving events. Most new gymnasts want to try the bars. It looks like a lot of fun. It is like being a monkey. You just swing from limb to limb.

A gymnast prepares to go from the lower bar to the higher one. Notice that her eyes are fixed on the high bar.

But most girls are surprised by the bars. The high bar is over 7 feet (2 m) off the floor. Who can ever reach it? The lower bar is just 5 feet (1.5 m) high. This is where your bar work will begin. You will learn simple pullovers. Then leg circles. Before you know it, that high bar will be in your hands.

See the chalk in a box by the bars? It is for your hands and thighs. Chalk absorbs sweat. It makes for smooth contact with the bar. It helps prevent hand blisters. Use plenty of chalk. Give your hands a chance to harden. Soon you will have calluses. They are the badge of a real gymnast.

Karen McMullin
performs a handstand
on the high bar
of the uneven bars.

THE POMMEL HORSE

Not many spectators like the horse. They think it is boring. It isn't dangerous like the high bar. And there is no big dismount at the end. In contests, the pommel horse comes after the floor exercises. The crowds love the floor work. It is exciting. Horse competition is quiet. It is not very flashy. But it is the hardest gymnastics event of all.

Why is the horse difficult? It requires great arm strength. But that is not the problem. It's the balance that's hard. All your weight is on your arms. Your legs must keep moving. They cannot touch the horse. Your legs make circles. You shift your weight from hand to hand. One slip and you are finished.

**Bart Conner displays
great arm strength
on the pommel horse.**

Kurt Thomas has made the horse more popular. He invented a new trick. It is called the Thomas Flair. Many gymnasts do it now. Thomas can even do it on the floor.

You will learn the horse in stages. First just try supporting yourself. Support yourself on the pommels. (They are the loops of wood on top.) Are you strong enough? Next you will learn to travel. That is moving along the horse. Then you will learn to swing your legs. Your legs will touch the horse at first. Don't be discouraged. Horse work is slow. It takes patience. It isn't for the show-off.

Brian Meeker's legs fly high over the horse.

THE RINGS

The ring routines used to be all strength. It took musclemen to do them. Back then gymnasts did pose after pose. They did Iron Crosses. They did Levers. They did Planches. Those are all strength moves. They are also crowd-pleasing moves.

Gymnasts still do the strength moves. But now they do more. They swing as well. Swinging is not easy. The rings want to move with you. But the rings must not swing. Only the body swings. And the whole body must swing. It looks exhausting. It is.

Kurt Thomas goes into an Iron Cross on the ring.

It is hard to hold the rings still. They want to go every which way. A handstand on the floor is simple. The floor does not move. The same is true for the parallel bars. They are not going anywhere. A handstand on the rings is not easy. Those rings just want to fly away from you.

Practice swinging on the rings. Remember, keep the rings still. Just swing your body from the wrists down.

Your coach will lower the rings. Now try hanging upside down. You will feel unsteady at first. Make sure someone spots you.

Try a straight-arm support. Your arms will wobble a lot. Everyone's do at first. You must hold the rings steady. Try to keep the rings in. Keep them close to your body. Strength is important. But so is balance. The rings require both.

Roger Palasson
does a perfect L-seat
on the rings.

THE PARALLEL BARS

Most gymnasts love the parallel bars. (They call them p-bars.) The p-bars use skills you have learned elsewhere. Tumbling skills are used. High bar and ring skills are used. Pommel horse and vaulting skills are used.

Gymnasts feel fairly safe on the p-bars. They are only 5½ feet (1.7 m) high. And there are two of them to hold onto. The rings and the high bar are 3 feet (1 m) higher.

But work on the p-bars takes some care. As with rings, you must learn to swing. You must swing your whole body. On p-bars that means swinging from the shoulders.

Start with your arms on top of the bars. Support is under your upper arm. Now swing. At first you will swing from the hips. Try not to. Swing from the shoulders. Keep the body in a straight line.

Jim Hartung does an aerial turn on the parallel bars.

Try swinging from a straight-arm support. Go slowly at first. Have someone spot you. Can you hold yourself up? You will build strength each practice.

During practice the bars may be lowered. This makes spotting easier. You will learn the shoulder stand. It looks great, and it is not too hard. You will also learn to roll on the bars.

Once gymnasts did handstand after handstand on the p-bars. Now the moves are very daring and original. Gymnasts often work a single bar. They release and regrasp the bars. They think up new ways to mount and dismount.

**Kurt Thomas uses
one of the
parallel bars to
show his strength
and skill.**

THE HIGH BAR

A young man goes to the bar. He chalks his hands and adjusts his grips. He looks up at the bar. It is 8½ feet (2.5 m) above the floor. The coach lifts while the gymnast jumps. Then the gymnast is on his own.

Quickly he is going fast around the bar. The Giant Swings are thrilling. Now he reverses them. Suddenly he lets go. The crowd holds its breath. The gymnast sails over the bar, turning. He regrips the bar. Now he is swinging forward again. The crowd cheers.

Beginners don't start with Giant Swings. First you must learn little swings. The bar will be lowered for you. Your swings will be slow. You will learn different ways to grip the bar. You will learn to release and regrip the bar.

Your coach will lower the bar some more. He will show you simple pullovers. Hip circles might be next. Soon you will be spinning around the bar. The wind will whistle in your ears.

And you will whistle to yourself as you leave the gym. You'll whistle a happy tune because gymnastics is so much fun!

WORDS GYMNASTS USE

Cast-off: A bar move. This involves changing from small circles to Giant Swings.

Grips: Handguards made of leather. They fit over the middle two fingers. They fasten around the wrist with straps.

Hip circles: Front or back circles on a bar. Legs are behind the bar.

Iron Cross: A strength move on the rings. The gymnast holds the rings out from his body. His arms and torso form a cross.

L-seat: A Half-Lever. The gymnast's body forms an L.

Leg circles: Front or back circles on a bar. The legs straddle the bar.

Lever: A strength move on the rings. The body is held parallel to the floor. It is below the level of the rings.

Planche: A strength move on the rings. The body is held parallel to the floor. It is above the level of the rings.

Pullover: A bar move. The gymnast pulls his body over and around a bar.

Spotting: Helping a gymnast perform a trick. This is done for the gymnast's safety.

Squat Vault: A simple vault. The gymnast clears the horse in a squat position.

Thomas Flair: A pommel horse trick. It was invented by Kurt Thomas, an American gymnast. The legs circle about the head in a precise pattern.

Tsukahara (tsoo-ka-HA-ra)**:** A very difficult vault. It is named for its inventor, a famous Japanese gymnast.

Walkover: A tumbling move. The gymnast moves his or her body forward, places hands down, and moves feet over head into a backbend. Then the gymnast returns to a standing position.

INDEX